Workbook

Economic Education for Consumers

THIRD EDITION

Roger LeRoy Miller

Alan D. Stafford

SOUTH-WESTERN
CENGAGE Learning™

Australia • Brazil • Japan • Korea • Mexico • Singapore • Spain • United Kingdom • United States

SOUTH-WESTERN
CENGAGE Learning™

Workbook: Economic Education for Consumers, Third Edition
Roger LeRoy Miller, Allan D. Stafford

VP/Editorial Director: Jack W. Calhoun

VP/Editor-in-Chief: Karen Schmohe

Acquisitions Editor: Marilyn Hornsby

Project Manager: Enid Nagel

Production Manager: Patricia Matthews Boies

Ancillary Coordinator: Kelly Resch

VP/Director of Marketing: Carol Volz

Senior Marketing Manager: Nancy Long

Marketing Coordinator: Angela A. Russo

Editorial Assistant: Linda Keith

Manufacturing Coordinator: Kevin Kluck

Art Director: Stacy Jenkins Shirley

For product information and technology assistance, contact us at
Cengage Learning Customer & Sales Support, 1-800-354-9706

For permission to use material from this text or product,
submit all requests online at **www.cengage.com/permissions**
Further permissions questions can be emailed to
permissionrequest@cengage.com

ISBN-13: 978-0-538-44113-1

ISBN-10: 0-538-44113-5

South-Western
5191 Natorp Boulevard
Mason, OH 45040
USA

Cengage Learning is a leading provider of customized learning solutions with office locations around the globe, including Singapore, the United Kingdom, Australia, Mexico, Brazil, and Japan. Locate your local office at **www.cengage.com/global**

Cengage Learning products are represented in Canada by Nelson Education, Ltd.

To learn more about South-Western, visit **www.cengage.com/southwestern**

Purchase any of our products at your local college store or at our preferred online store **www.ichapters.com**

Printed in the United States of America
4 5 6 7 8   13 12 11 10 09

ED229

Economic Education for Consumers
Workbook

Contents

Chapter 1 Consumers—The Engine that Runs the Economy

1.1 Decisions, Decisions

Key Terms Review

Define each of the following vocabulary terms.

1. values_____

2. goals_____

3. needs_____

4. wants_____

5. opportunity cost_____

_____

Concepts Review

6. What power does the consumer have over businesses?

_____

_____

7. What are the differences between life, work, and social values?

_____

_____

8. Describe, in your own words, the meaning of *life span* and *life cycle* and how these terms are related to each other.

_____

_____

9. Explain the difference between a need and a want. Give an example of each.

_____

_____

_____

_____

Critical Thinking

10. Why is it important to consider opportunity costs when you make a decision?

_____

_____

11. Explain how your short-term goals should be related to your life-span goals?

_____

_____

Consumer Applications

12. Gina went to her local mall with her friends. The mall is huge and has many options from which to choose. She has $50 that she can spend. There are so many things she wants to buy. For instance, a department store in the mall is having a sale on jeans. Gina has jeans, but they're kind of old. She also knows that she will need a new backpack for next semester, because hers will hardly hold her books anymore. Write a suggestion for Gina.

_____

_____

_____

_____

_____

Chapter 1 Consumers—The Engine that Runs the Economy

1.2 Make Decisions

#1-7 ABSENT

Key Terms Review

Define each of the following vocabulary terms.

1. rational buying decision *a choice made in an organized, logical manor.*

2. impulse purchase *a purchase made on a whim w/ out using the dec. making process*

Concepts Review

3. If you wanted to buy a Digital Video Diskette (DVD) player, would this most likely be a rational buying decision or impulse purchase? Why?

   Rational b/c there are many diff. manufac. & they differ in what they do. It's also a more expensive purchase & requires more thought & analysis to be impulsive.

4. Give an example of an impulse purchase.

   Buying gum/candy/pop/or magazines while checking out

5. What could be a disadvantage of an impulse purchase?

   You could miss an opp. to get a better deal or could then limit/you prevent yourself from being able to buy ol'teke you want

6. Write the step that identifies the decision making process next to the letter.

   Search   a. Research on the Internet, read, talk to salespeople and bicyclists.

   Specify   b. Deciding whether or not you should buy a new mountain bike.

Study

Sift

Select

c. After buying the bicycle, take it on a mountain trail.

d. Test ride bikes at different stores, considering price and service.

e. Choosing a bicycle and buying it.

7. Put the steps in exercise 6 in the correct order.

    B , A , D , e , C

Critical Thinking

8. Give an example of two people who can have the same values but different goals.

    _____

    _____

    _____

9. Jerediel and Shane each have $75 and want to buy portable CD players. After considering the features and prices of several players, Shane chose to buy a less expensive model than the one Jerediel purchased. What are the benefits and opportunity costs of Shane's decision?

    _____

    _____

Consumer Applications

10. You are considering buying three compact disks over the Internet. The price is $13.99 for each compact disk plus $3.00 for shipping and handling. At the discount superstore, the compact disks are $14.49 each. How much money will you save with less expensive option? What is the benefit and opportunity cost of each option?

    _____

    _____

    _____

    _____

    _____

4

Chapter 1 Consumers—The Engine that Runs the Economy

1.3 Understand Economic Systems

Key Terms Review

Define each of the following vocabulary terms.

1. economic system _____

2. production _____

3. resources _____

4. economics _____

5. traditional economy _____

6. command economy _____

_____

7. capitalist or market economy _____

_____

8. profit _____

_____

9. mixed economy _____

Concepts Review

10. Give an example of a "good" and a "service." What kind of business would offer both?

_____

_____

11. A farmer is told what to grow, how much to grow, and for how much to sell it. What kind of economy would this be?

_____

12. Give examples of human and nonhuman resources.

_____

_____

13. In a pure market economy, with no government interference, do you think automobile manufacturers would meet the safety standards they do now? Explain your answer.

_____

14. List three businesses that are subject to at least some government control.

_____

_____

Critical Thinking

15. You decide to open up your own pet-grooming business. What resources do you need to get started? What costs do you need to consider for setting prices?

_____

_____

16. What economic situation exists when a business is able to sell exactly as many products as it is able to produce?

_____

_____

Consumer Applications

17. Kiara took her car to her mechanic for an oil change. The price of the service had increased dramatically from when she had it done three months earlier. When she asked for an explanation, the mechanic told her that the government had passed new regulations regarding the disposal of oil. Why do you think these new regulations cost the consumer more money? How does the consumer benefit from these regulations?

_____

_____

_____

_____

Chapter 1 Consumers—The Engine that Runs the Economy

1.4 Consumer's Role in the Economy

Key Terms Review

Define each of the following vocabulary terms.

1. consumer_____

2. consumer economics_____

3. consumer sovereignty_____

Concepts Review

4. What information does a consumer provide to a producer of goods or services? How is this information provided?

    _____

    _____

5. What is the most important reason to run a business in a market economy?

    _____

    _____

6. Define competition in your own words.

    _____

    _____

7. How does the consumer affect competition?

    _____

    _____

    _____

    _____

Critical Thinking

8. Tony's Pizzeria is across the street from an office building. Tony's does a lot of lunch business during the week, but on weekends, it is very slow. It is not in the center of town or near any shopping centers. How could Tony increase his weekend sales?

_____

_____

9. Taco Juan's is a very popular fast-food restaurant, but it is barely making a profit. Juan has an all-you-can-eat daily lunch buffet. He cannot serve the leftover food for dinner, so whatever he doesn't sell has to be thrown away. Juan has several people working for him and does not want anyone to lose their job. The restaurant's hours are from 11 A.M. to 11 P.M. How can Juan increase his efficiency and his profits?

_____

_____

_____

Consumer Applications

10. Your friend's father owns a sporting goods store. Though the merchandise is top quality and you would like to shop there to support his business, his prices are very high. You can buy the same merchandise in a chain store in the mall and spend a lot less money. Why do you think his prices are so high? How would you let your friend know that his father's store is too expensive? Where would you shop and why?

_____

_____

_____

_____

_____

_____

Chapter 1 Consumers—The Engine that Runs the Economy

1.5 Advertising and Consumer Decisions

Key Terms Review

Define each of the following vocabulary terms.

1. brand advertising _causes you 2 remember a port. brand_

2. informative advertising _is designed to influence you to buy a product by educ. you about the prod. benefit._

3. comparative advertising _wins favor by comparing its product's qualities of those comp. products._

illegal

4. defensive advertising _counterattacks from comp. ads._

5. persuasive advertising _appeal to emotions to buy-not inf._

6. deceptive advertising _cont. fact. wrong statements_

7. puffery _distinguish innocent exaggeration._

legal

Concepts Review _loss liter item priced bellow value to get you into the store._

8. Are brand name products always better quality? Why do they cost more than unfamiliar or store brands?

_____

_____

9. What is the difference between deceptive advertising and puffery?

_____

_____

_____

10. Match the slogan with the type of advertising listed below.

(A) brand (B) informative (C) comparative (D) defensive (E) persuasive

_____ *Fresh* deodorant—You'll feel Fresh all day long!

_____ *Wagner's* Extra Crunchy Chips are best for dips!

_____ *Al's Healthful Subs* have fewer calories than *Nero's Subs*!

_____ *Nero's* subs have 50 percent more calories than Al's subs because they are 50 percent larger than Al's subs. Don't be fooled by false claims!

_____ *Your Neighborhood Bank*—Our low interest home-equity loan offers no closing costs and no application fees.

Critical Thinking

11. Why do you think deceptive advertising is illegal?

_____

_____

_____

12. When a celebrity endorses a product, what kind of advertising is this? Explain your answer.

_____

_____

Consumer Applications

13. Suzanne saw an ad on TV for a new perfume. It portrayed a woman who walked into a crowded room and everyone wanted to be near her because of the perfume. When she bought the perfume and wore it to a party, she was disappointed. What kind of advertisement was this? How could Suzanne have avoided her disappointment?

_____

_____

_____

_____

Chapter 1 Consumers—The Engine that Runs the Economy

1.6 Be a Responsible Consumer

Concepts Review

1. Name three natural resources that you use as an individual consumer.

    _____

2. Is water a need or a want? How is water wasted?

    _____

    _____

3. Is oil a need or a want? How is oil wasted?

    _____

    _____

4. If you are wasteful of natural resources, how does it affect others?

    _____

    _____

5. How can you, as a consumer, encourage businesses to act socially responsible?

    _____

    _____

6. How does your local or federal government help conserve resources and preserve the environment?

    _____

    _____

    _____

    _____

Critical Thinking

7. Why do you think it is important for consumers to support environmentally responsible businesses?

_____

_____

8. Why do you think the government often provides funding to cities building mass transit systems?

_____

_____

_____

Consumer Applications

9. Melika is buying a telephone. There are two models that she is interested in buying. The less expensive one has a lot of packaging which includes quite a bit of Styrofoam, plastic wrap, and cardboard. Melika is concerned about the environment. Should she send the manufacturer a message by not buying the excessive packaging, or should she save herself several dollars and hope that somebody else will send the message?

_____

_____

_____

Chapter 2   Buying Technology Products—Let's Talk Tech

2.1 Technology and Consumer Choice

Key Terms Review

Define each of the following vocabulary terms.

1. technological obsolescence_____

_____

2. depreciation_____

Concepts Review

3. How have technological changes affected consumer decisions?

_____

4. What sources are available for obtaining information about technology-based products?

_____

_____

_____

5. Why is it difficult to decide when to buy technology-based products?

_____

6. Why do companies charge a high price for new technology-based products?

_____

_____

_____

7. What are some of the reasons to wait to buy technology-based products?

_____

_____

Critical Thinking

8. Do you think companies ever plan for their product to be obsolete? Why?

   _____

   _____

   _____

9. What factors will you consider when buying a new-technology product?

   _____

   _____

   _____

Consumer Applications

10. Jacques has a large collection of music CDs. Each week he adds to his collection. His CD player has stopped working, and he is considering buying a new one that also plays DVDs that he could watch on his TV. Jacques has many VCR tapes but owns no DVDs. The new player costs $250, but he could simply replace his CD player for about $100. Should Jacques purchase the new technology? What factors should he consider as he makes his decision?

   _____

   _____

   _____

   _____

   _____

   _____

   _____

   _____

   _____

Chapter 2   Buying Technology Products—Let's Talk Tech

2.2 Move Into Cyberspace

Key Terms Review

Define each of the following vocabulary terms.

1. Internet_____

    _____

2. HyperText Markup Language (HTML)_____

    _____

3. World Wide Web (WWW)_____

    _____

4. Web browser_____

5. modern_____

    _____

6. Internet service provider (ISP)_____

    _____

Concepts Review

7. Why was the Internet started?

    _____

    _____

8. What are two ways to connect to the Internet?

    _____

    _____

9. How can you find out if an ISP can get you on the Internet anytime you want?

_____

_____

10. Why is the location of an ISP that communicates over telephone lines important?

_____

_____

Critical Thinking

11. Why do you think the Internet has become so popular?

_____

_____

_____

12. What considerations other than immediate access and local access phone numbers should consumers consider when choosing an ISP?

_____

_____

Consumer Applications

13. Kuniko wants to choose an Internet service provider. There are many available, but she has narrowed her choice to three alternatives. One is a national ISP that offers her unlimited use over telephone lines for $23 per month. The second is a local provider that also provides unlimited access over telephone lines but for $14.99 per month. Her final choice is a·cable DSL link that is much faster than either of the other ISPs. It would cost $48.99 each month. Kuniko is on a "tight" budget but wants to be able to surf the net without having to wait to move from screen to screen. Which service would you recommend she choose and why?

_____

_____

_____

_____

Chapter 2   Buying Technology Products—Let's Talk Tech

2.3 Choose a Personal Computer

Key Terms Review

Define each of the following vocabulary terms.

1. central processing unit (CPU)_____

    _____

2. microprocessors_____

    _____

3. random access memory (RAM)_____

    _____

4. hard drive_____

5. CD-ROM_____

6. DVD-ROM_____

7. peripheral device_____

8. laptop or notebook computer_____

Concepts Review

9. What should a consumer consider before going computer shopping?

    _____

    _____

10. What is the importance of RAM?

    _____

11. What types of data storage are available on personal computers?

    _____

12. What are some of the reasons to consider buying a laptop computer?

_____

_____

Critical Thinking

13. Do you think that a computer you buy today will be useful in three years? Why or why not?

_____

_____

14. Why do laptop computers cost 50 to 75 percent more than desktop computers?

_____

_____

_____

_____

Consumer Applications

15. Michelle is attending college and is majoring in engineering. She has been using the computers on campus to run programs that solve complex mathematical calculations, connect to the Internet to do research, and write her term papers. She has decided to purchase a computer of her own so that she does not have to spend so much time on campus. What do you think are Michelle's most important considerations in purchasing this new computer?

_____

_____

_____

_____

_____

_____

Chapter 2   Buying Technology Products—Let's Talk Tech

2.4 Shop on the Net

Concepts Review

1. What are some advantages and disadvantages of shopping on the Internet?

    _____

    _____

    _____

    _____

2. Why can an Internet retailer offer many more styles and sizes than a retail store?

    _____

    _____

3. What types of problems might result from providing personal and credit card information when ordering on the Internet?

    _____

    _____

    _____

4. Why do banks provide online services?

    _____

    _____

5. Why are businesses willing to pay for Internet advertising?

    _____

6. Why do most businesses maintain a web site?

    _____

    _____

Critical Thinking

7. Why do you think Internet retailers have lower costs than a retail store?

_____

_____

_____

8. Do you think it costs more to advertise on a popular web site? Why?

_____

_____

_____

Consumer Applications

The chart below shows the pricing structure for a comparable pair of hiking boots offered by four different companies.

Company	Retail Price	Web Price
B.B. Strong	$82.00	$78.00
Water's Edge	$93.00	$89.00
Nature Unlimited	$77.00	$74.00
Freddie Power	$86.00	$81.00

9. What is the average retail price and the average web price?

_____

_____

_____

10. For each pair of boots, calculate how much the consumer will save by buying the boots on the Web. What is the percentage savings of each?

_____

_____

_____

Chapter 2   Buying Technology Products—Let's Talk Tech

2.5 Protect Yourself on the Internet

Key Terms Review

Define each of the following vocabulary terms.

1. cookies_____

2. spam_____

Concepts Review

3. Why is it necessary to take precautions to protect your privacy when you use the Internet?

   _____

   _____

4. What are some of the ways to control the risk of cookies?

   _____

   _____

   _____

5. What are some of the ways to investigate whether or not an offer for prizes or free luxury items on the Internet is legitimate?

   _____

   _____

   _____

6. What types of organizations may send out spam?

   _____

   _____

   _____

Critical Thinking

7. What types of organizations may be interested in obtaining your personal data? Why?

    _____

    _____

    _____

8. Do you think the advantages of cookies are greater than the disadvantages? Why or why not?

    _____

    _____

    _____

Consumer Applications

9. Consuelo enjoyed surfing the Internet and frequently visited the web sites of the investment companies with whom she had accounts. Not long after she had opened a new account, she began receiving spam that contained offers from financial planners, real estate brokers, credit card companies, and travel resorts. What type of information do you think these organizations had obtained about Consuelo? Some of the offers she received were attractive. What action should she take?

    _____

    _____

    _____

    _____

    _____

    _____

    _____

    _____

    _____

Chapter 3 Consumer Protection—Rights, Responsibilities, Resolution

3.1 Consumer Rights and Responsibilities

Key Terms Review   #2-6

Define each of the following vocabulary terms.

1. competition *contest among sellers to win cust.*

2. monopoly *A company which had an unfair advantage of comp. in an area q business.*

Concepts Review

3. How does a monopoly violate the consumer's Right to Choose?

   B/c it cripples the variety of manuf. / comp. of which to choose from

4. If a newly installed air-conditioner shorts out and a fire results, what right and responsibility does the consumer have?

   The right to insurance (sue), inv. a resp. to developer authority- the guy yep.

5. In New Jersey, a developer built a community on land that was once used as a dump for chemical waste. What consumer right could the developer have violated?

   The right to be safe. (heathy env.)

6. A man reaches into a snowblower as it was running to get a rock that was wedged in the blades. He is badly cut. Is the snowblower unsafe?

   No, the mans an idiot. Shouldn't put your hand in a running snowblower.

7. When a legislative body is considering consumer interests, how would they know what issues to address to create the necessary laws?

_____

_____

_____

Critical Thinking

8. A consumer purchased carpeting, had it installed, and later was dissatisfied because it was not treated with stain-resistant chemicals. How could this have been avoided?

_____

_____

_____

_____

9. Why do you think it is the consumer's responsibility to seek redress?

_____

_____

_____

Consumer Applications

10. Eric saw an advertisement at a local car dealership that offered financing for used cars at a very low interest rate. When he went there, the saleswoman kept promising him the advertised rate. He found a car he liked, but when he and the saleswoman were filling out the forms for a loan, she told him that the interest rate advertised did not apply to the car that he wanted. Which of the Consumer Bill of Rights was violated, and why? What are Eric's responsibilities?

_____

_____

_____

_____

Chapter 3 Consumer Protection—Rights, Responsibilities, Resolution

3.2 Government and Consumer Protection

Key Terms Review

Define or describe the function of the following vocabulary terms.

1. consumer movement_____

   _____

2. Federal Trade Commission_____

   _____

3. cease-and-desist order_____

4. Consumer Product Safety Commission (CPSC)_____

   _____

5. Environmental Protection Agency (EPA)_____

6. warranty_____

   _____

7. full warrranty_____

   _____

8. limited warranty_____

9. implied warranty_____

   _____

Concepts Review

10. What was the intention of the Interstate Commerce Act of 1887?

   _____

11. What are the FTC's responsibilities?

_____

_____

_____

12. In 1975, the Magnuson-Moss Warranty Act was passed. What was wrong with warranties prior to 1975?

_____

_____

Critical Thinking

13. Why do you suppose that the consumer movement needed the government to intervene on behalf of the consumer? Why don't the businesses regulate themselves?

_____

_____

_____

14. What does a warranty say about a company's confidence in their product?

_____

_____

Consumer Applications

15. Lorena bought two new tires for her car at $90.00 each. The tires were warranteed for 50,000 miles. If there was any defect or early wear, then the percentage of mileage remaining would be applied toward the price of new tires. After 40,000 miles, the tires needed to be replaced, but now the tires cost $110.00 each. How much does Lorena have to pay for her new tires?

_____

_____

_____

Chapter 3 Consumer Protection—Rights, Responsibilities, Resolution

3.3 Deception and Fraud   —Absent—

Key Terms Review

Define each of the following vocabulary terms.

1. trading up _trying to get you to buy_
    sell you more expensive (upgrade)

2. loss leader _priced bellow cost to lure you in_

3. fraud _deliberate deception (illegal)_

4. bait and switch _get cust. in with an adv. product_
    thats not there + try to get you to get another.

5. pyramid scheme _selling memberships_
    fake memberships.

Concepts Review

6. Give two examples each of deception and fraud.

    _____

7. What is a sale price?
    price bellow the usual price

8. What is the difference between "trading up" and "bait and switch"?
    Trading up is a little manipulative
    but its legal while bait'n'switch
    is both manip. & illegal.

9. How can a "loss leader" be deceptive?

_____

_____

10. Who profits in a pyramid scheme?

_____

11. How does the telephone offer advantages to would-be con artists?

Not able to virually sale & prevent my not be legit.

Critical Thinking

12. If a business did not have the item that was advertised, what steps could it take to avoid being accused of practicing "bait and switch"?

_____

_____

13. Why do you think a "loss leader" can financially hurt a competing business?

_____

_____

Consumer Applications

14. Scott brought his 1965 Ford Mustang to Honest John's to be restored. John gave him an estimate for materials and labor. When Scott dropped the car off, John demanded the money for all of the materials and half the labor. What should Scott do?

_____

_____

_____

_____

Chapter 3   Consumer Protection—Rights, Responsibilities, Resolution

3.4 Resolve Consumer Problems

Key Terms Review

Define each of the following vocabulary terms.

1. Better Business Bureau_____

_____

_____

_____

_____

2. cooling-off period_____

_____

3. small claims court_____

_____

Concepts Review

4. What documentation is necessary to begin a complaint process?

_____

5. Write the five (5) facts you should list when describing the situation surrounding your complaint?

_____

_____

_____

_____

6. In your own words, what is a "cooling-off period" and how long does it usually last?

_____

_____

_____

7. Does a small-claims court collect the judgment if you win?

_____

_____

8. What are some government efforts to help consumers?

_____

_____

Critical Thinking

9. Why should you never relinquish any original documents while pursuing your complaint?

_____

_____

_____

_____

Consumer Applications

10. Yvonne purchased a portable stereo. After one week, the CD player portion of the stereo stopped working. How should Yvonne go about the complaint process? What remedy should she ask for?

_____

_____

_____

_____

Chapter 4   Choose A Career—Get A Job

4.1 Get To Know Yourself

Key Terms Review

Define each of the following vocabulary terms.

1. personal interests_____

2. aptitude_____

3. transferable skill_____

4. personality_____

_____

Concepts Review

5. What do you need to know about yourself to make useful career plans?

_____

6. To make a good career choice, what must you understand about yourself?

_____

7. How do you determine your interests?

_____

8. Your interests may lead you toward particular careers, but what does success in a career require?

_____

9. What are some ways to identify one's personality?

_____

_____

_____

Critical Thinking

10. If you were to put the ten values listed in your book in order of importance, what would be the first three? What would be the last three? What does this say about yourself?

_____

_____

_____

11. Explain how your career choice is likely to affect other members of your family at the present and in the future.

_____

_____

_____

12. What personality type (listed in your book) do you think you have? Does this fit with your aptitudes? Do you think someone who is creative would more likely have a verbal aptitude or a numerical aptitude? Why?

_____

_____

_____

Consumer Applications

13. Jose has always done well in art. He has won several area contests and taken many art courses in high school, but he's not sure what his career choice will be after high school. His father is a plumber and would like Jose to join him in the family's business. His mother is an accountant and wants Jose to go to the same college as she did. Jose is not sure of what he should do. What would you tell Jose?

_____

_____

_____

_____

Chapter 4   Choose A Career—Get A Job

4.2 Explore Careers

Key Terms Review

Define each of the following vocabulary terms.

1. job_____

2. career_____

Concepts Review

3. List five federal sources of career information.

   _____

   _____

4. List the four private sources of career information.

   _____

   _____

5. What is the function of a private employment agency?

   _____

   _____

6. How do you plan for your career?

   _____

   _____

   _____

7. What are some financial considerations in planning your career?

   _____

   _____

Critical Thinking

8. In your own words, what is the difference between a career and a job?

_____

_____

_____

9. What are the advantages and disadvantages of making a *career connection* with someone who works in the field in which you're interested as a career?

_____

_____

_____

_____

_____

_____

_____

Consumer Applications

10. Denzel is a senior in high school who excels in mathematics. He would like to be a high school math teacher. Where would Denzel get information on this career? What planning is involved?

_____

_____

_____

_____

_____

_____

_____

Chapter 4   Choose a Career—Get a Job

4.3 Apply for a Job

Key Terms Review

Define each of the following vocabulary terms.

1. referral _____

_____

2. temporary agencies _____

_____

3. resume _____

4. cover letter _____

5. references _____

_____

Concepts Review

6. What kind of jobs are you most likely to find in the newspaper's help-wanted ads?

_____

7. What information should you find out before enlisting the service of a private employment agency?

_____

8. What are the advantages and disadvantages of accepting work from a tem-porary agency?

_____

_____

_____

_____

9. What is the advantage of having a resume over filling out a job application?

_____

Critical Thinking

10. What could be another reason, other than the one discussed in your textbook, why most employers do not advertise their job openings.

_____

_____

_____

_____

11. Why is it important to include your extracurricular activities, volunteer work, and any special honors on your resume?

_____

_____

_____

Consumer Applications

12. Elena has an excellent relationship with her employer. A friend of a friend asked her for a referral for a job where she worked. She has met this person a few times but doesn't know her very well. How would you advise Elena on her decision?

_____

_____

_____

_____

_____

_____

_____

_____

Chapter 4   Choose A Career—Get A Job

4.4 Interview Successfully

Key Terms Review

Define each of the following vocabulary terms.

1. interview_____

Concepts Review

2. Why is the interview important for both you and the employer?

_____

_____

_____

3. Why is being prompt to the interview essential?

_____

_____

_____

4. Why would you bring a few extra copies of your resume to the interview?

_____

_____

_____

5. What are some questions that employers aren't allowed to ask?

_____

_____

_____

_____

Critical Thinking

6. If an employer asks an applicant what they liked least about a job, what are some answers that could be given? What are some answers that should not be given?

_____

_____

_____

_____

7. If an employer asked you a question to which you didn't know the answer, how should you respond?

_____

_____

_____

8. Why do you think it is illegal to ask a woman if she is planning to have children?

_____

_____

_____

_____

Consumer Applications

9. Brian lost his previous job after he refused his boss's request to falsify documents. Brian knew that he would not be able to use his boss as a reference, yet he didn't know how to respond on an interview when asked why he left his last job. How should Brian answer?

_____

_____

_____

_____

Chapter 4   Choose A Career—Get A Job

4.5 Prepare for the Future

Key Terms Review

Define each of the following vocabulary terms.

1. downsizing_____

2. severance pay_____

3. notice_____

Concepts Review

4. What does success in your first job provide?

   _____

5. What are some reasons why people change careers?

   _____

   _____

   _____

6. If you are terminated due to downsizing, why should you be sure to get a written recommendation?

   _____

   _____

7. What should you do if you are unable to solve your problems on the job?

   _____

8. What qualifications do you need to consider if you would like to change your career or profession?

   _____

   _____

Critical Thinking

9. Why should you always keep your resume up to date, even if you're currently employed?

_____

_____

_____

_____

10. If a supervisor had to downsize her department and had to choose among her equally qualified employees, on what basis could she make her decision on whom to keep?

_____

_____

_____

_____

Consumer Applications

11. Mary had been a salesclerk in the mall for more than a year when she learned of another job that offered better pay. She applied for the job, and when it was offered to her on Tuesday, the new employer asked if she could start next Monday. What should Mary do?

_____

_____

_____

_____

_____

_____

_____

Chapter 5   Income Taxes—How Much Will You Keep?

5.1 Taxes and Your Paycheck

Key Terms Review

Define each of the following vocabulary terms.

1. payroll taxes_____

2 income tax_____

   _____

3. Federal Insurance Contributions Act (FICA)_____

   _____

4. withholding_____

5. gross income_____

6. net income_____

   _____

7. Form W-4_____

   _____

8. Internal Revenue Service (IRS)_____

9. allowance_____

Concepts Review

10. Why do employers withhold taxes every paycheck rather than all at once at the end of the year?

   _____

   _____

   _____

11. What are some factors affecting the amount of income tax you owe?

_____

_____

12. How do you know how many allowances you should claim?

_____

13. Does the number of allowances you claim change the amount you owe? Why or why not?

_____

_____

_____

14. How can you avoid paying a large tax bill, and maybe a fine, at the end of the year?

_____

_____

Critical Thinking

15. Why is it a bad decision to claim too few allowances during the year so you can have a large refund at the end of the year?

_____

_____

_____

Consumer Applications

16. Allison worked 30 hours last week at $7.00 hour. Her federal income tax withholding was $22.00. Her state income tax withholding was $7.15. With FICA at 6.20 percent and Medicare tax at 1.45 percent, what was her net pay?

_____

_____

_____

Chapter 5   Income Taxes—How Much Will You Keep?

5.2 File a Tax Return

Key Terms Review

Define each of the following vocabulary terms.

1. tax return_____

2. Form W-2_____

3. Form 1099-INT_____

4. Form 1040-EZ_____

5. dependent_____

6. deductions_____

   _____

7. Social Security number_____

   _____

8. taxable income_____

Concepts Review

9. What is considered income?

   _____

10. What qualifies you to use form 1040EZ?

   _____

   _____

   _____

   _____

   _____

11. What is the benefit of filing Form 1040?

_____

_____

_____

Critical Thinking

12. Why do you think employers have a deadline of January 31 to mail their employees a W-2 form?

_____

_____

_____

13. Why would you deposit your refund electronically?

_____

_____

_____

Consumer Applications

14. Nathan is single. He earned $33,828 in wages plus $186 in interest last year. The standard deduction for a single person is $7,800. His employer withheld $3,756 from his pay. (a) What was his adjusted gross income? (b) What was his taxable income? (c) What amount of tax did he owe (use the tax table in your text)? (d) How large was his refund?

_____

_____

_____

_____

Chapter 5   Income Taxes—How Much Will You Keep?

5.3 Taxes and Government

Key Terms Review

Define each of the following vocabulary terms.

1. sales taxes_____

   _____

2. property taxes_____

3. excise tax_____

   _____

4. estate taxes_____

   _____

5. gift taxes_____

6. business or license tax_____

7. customs duties or tariffs_____

Concepts Review

8. How does the government receive money?

    _____

9. From where does the federal government receive the largest part of its income?

    _____

10. What are the three ways to classify taxes?

    _____

    _____

    _____

11. Define and give an example of the benefit principle of taxation.

_____

_____

12. What are the three ways that taxes are based on the share of income they take as people's incomes change?

_____

Critical Thinking

13. Why do you think states have a business or license tax for plumbers, barbers, electricians, and cosmetologists?

_____

_____

_____

_____

14. Is a benefit principle of taxation an example of a progressive tax or regressive tax? Explain your answer.

_____

_____

_____

_____

Consumer Applications

15. Your school is proposing a budget increase that would cost your family an additional $350 a year in taxes. If the proposal does not pass, it will be forced to reduce programs and supplies. Will you vote for or against the proposal? Explain your answer.

_____

_____

_____

Chapter 5   Income Taxes—How Much Will You Keep?

5.4 Government Spending

Key Terms Review

Define each of the following vocabulary terms.

1. public goods_____

_____

Concepts Review

2. How does the government use taxes to influence consumers' decisions?

_____

_____

3. What are the six major areas where your tax dollars are spent?

_____

_____

_____

_____

_____

4. Give three examples of the benefits state and local governments provide.

_____

_____

_____

_____

_____

_____

Critical Thinking

5. Some people feel that school taxes should be paid only by people who have children in the school system. What would happen to our schools if this were the case? How does education benefit all citizens?

_____

_____

_____

_____

_____

6. Some people believe taxes on tobacco products should be increased to discourage smoking. Discuss two costs and two benefits to the U.S. economy that might result from such a tax increase.

_____

_____

_____

_____

Consumer Applications

7. Jermaine drove to school this morning. Of the eight examples of what state and local goverments provide (listed in your textbook), how many affect him and how?

_____

_____

_____

_____

_____

_____

_____

Chapter 6   Budgeting—How Will You Use Your Money?

6.1 Choose Financial Goals

Key Terms Review

Define each of the following vocabulary terms.

1. budget _____

_____

2. short-term goals _____

3. life-span goals _____

_____

Concepts Review

4. What is the first step in the budgeting process?

_____

5. What are two types of financial goals?

_____

6. What is the difference between short-term and life-span financial goals?

_____

_____

_____

_____

7. What do you need to consider when choosing your short-terms goals?

_____

_____

_____

Critical Thinking

8. Why is it more difficult to plan life-span financial goals than short-term financial goals?

_____

_____

_____

_____

_____

9. When budgeting your finances for your short-term goals, what are some opportunity costs that may be involved?

_____

_____

_____

_____

Consumer Applications

10. David wants to become a chef after high school and own a restaurant someday. His parents cannot afford to send him to the cooking school he wants to attend next year. Currently, he is working in the kitchen of a local restaurant. How can David turn his job into a career and achieve both his short-term and life-span goals? How would his achievement benefit his community?

_____

_____

_____

_____

_____

_____

_____

Chapter 6   Budgeting—How Will You Use Your Money?

6.2 Track Income and Expenses

Key Terms Review

Define each of the following vocabulary terms.

1. fixed expenses _____

2. flexible expenses _____

3. luxury goods _____

_____

Concepts Review

4. In the budget process, what is the next step after determining your goals?

_____

_____

5. What items are included in your spending records?

_____

_____

6. What is necessary for effective record-keeping?

_____

_____

_____

7. What is an advantage of most fixed expenses?

_____

_____

_____

_____

Critical Thinking

8. Next to the items listed, write whether they are fixed or flexible expenses.

_____	weekly groceries	_____	car payment
_____	monthly rent	_____	long-distance telephone bill
_____	car insurance	_____	clothing
_____	monthly heating bill	_____	gasoline
_____	monthly cable bill	_____	daily newspaper delivery

9. Why do you need to categorize your spending records?

_____

_____

_____

_____

_____

Consumer Applications

10. Amin has saved $4,000 toward the purchase of a $6,000 used car he wants to buy. When he buys the car, he will also need $500 for his first insurance payment, $140 for his registration, and 6 percent of the car's price for sales tax. Amin is able to save $500 per month. When will he be able to pay cash for the car?

_____

_____

_____

_____

_____

_____

Chapter 6   Budgeting—How Will You Use Your Money?

6.3 Your Budget Worksheet

Key Terms Review

Define each of the following vocabulary terms.

1. budget worksheet_____

_____

Concepts Review

2. What information goes into your budget worksheet?

_____

_____

3. What does a budget worksheet show you?

_____

_____

4. What are the five steps in building a budget worksheet?

_____

_____

5. Why do many people give up on using a budget worksheet or not attempt to use one at all?

_____

_____

Critical Thinking

6. What does the statement, "Your income is a limited resource," mean?

_____

_____

_____

7. Why should saving be listed on the worksheet as an expense, and your spending be adjusted to achieve this goal?

_____

_____

_____

8. If your income was under (−) and your spending was over (+), what does that mean?

_____

_____

Consumer Applications

9. Ling created and implemented a monthly budget worksheet for herself.

Income
Paycheck (net) $150.00/week

Expenses
Eating out $25.00/week
Birthday gifts $75.00/month
Movies $15.00/week
Clothes $100.00/month
Personal care items $40.00/month

Savings   ?/month

Ling would like to save $400 per month. Calculate her monthly income, expenses, and current savings for a four-week period. Is she able to achieve her saving goal? How much over or under are her monthly savings? If you were Ling and your monthly expenses were less than you had expected, what would you do with the extra money? Would you add to your savings, or would you spend it? If Ling's savings are short of her goal, what types of spending would you recommend she reduce?

_____

_____

_____

_____

_____

_____

Chapter 6   Budgeting—How Will You Use Your Money?

6.4 Create Your Budget for the Year

Key Terms Review

Define each of the following vocabulary terms.

1. balanced budget_____

Concepts Review

2. What is the purpose of a budget worksheet?

_____

_____

_____

3. When you need to reduce spending, what expenses can you cut back on?

_____

_____

_____

4. If you spent more than you expected in month, what are your two options?

_____

_____

5. What is the purpose of a budget?

_____

_____

6. What is the purpose of reviewing your budget at least once a year?

_____

_____

_____

Critical Thinking

7. If your friend asked you to help her establish a budget and create a worksheet, with what parts can you help and why?

_____

_____

_____

_____

8. Why should you review your budget if you change your goals?

_____

_____

_____

9. How can a budget be your safeguard against having too much debt?

_____

_____

_____

Consumer Applications

10. Dina has saved $150 for a new mountain bike. Her parents agreed to help her earn the other $300 she needs by paying her to work around the house. They identified tasks she could do each month and how much she would earn per task. Dina has other expenses each month. Determine how long it will take her to earn the $300 she needs to buy the mountain bike

Tasks and Pay		Dina's Other Monthly Expenses	
Wash Windows	$25	Movies	$15
Clean Basement	20	Clothing	25
Baby sit brother	30	Eating out	10
Make father's lunch	10	Cosmetics	10
Wash family car	15	Art supplies	10

_____

_____

_____

_____

Chapter 7   Banking Services—Where To Stash Your Cash

7.1 How Banks Work

Key Terms Review

Define each of the following vocabulary terms.

1. purchasing power_____

2. Federal Deposit Insurance Corporation (FDIC)_____

    _____

3. barter_____

4. currency_____

5. check_____

    _____

6. payee_____

7. statement_____

Concepts Review

8. Why do banks charge borrowers a higher rate of interest than they pay their depositors?

    _____

9. What are some of the reasons to deposit your money in a bank?

    _____

10. What is the function of the FDIC?

    _____

    _____

    _____

11. How do banks make our communities better places to live?

_____

_____

_____

12. What are the advantages of using checks?

_____

_____

_____

Critical Thinking

13. Why do you think that banks are regulated by the government?

_____

_____

_____

_____

14. Banks earn a profit by charging interest to borrowers. Why do you think they pay interest to depositors?

_____

_____

Consumer Applications

15. Your friend Jerry has just started a part-time job at a grocery store. He would like to save enough money to buy a car stereo and some new clothes for school. He doesn't have a bank account. How will you convince him to open an account.

_____

_____

_____

Chapter 7 Banking Services—Where To Stash Your Cash

7.2 Use Your Checking Account

Key Terms Review

Define each of the following vocabulary terms

1. checking account_____

   _____

2. check register_____

3. account balance_____

4. overdrawing_____

5. endorsement_____

6. third party checks_____

Concepts Review

7. What are the requirements for opening a checking account?

   _____

   _____

8. What are the parts of the check that must be filled out?

   _____

   _____

   _____

9. What must you do to cash a check?

   _____

   _____

   _____

10. If you have deposited a check into your account, why can't you immediately withdraw the money?

_____

_____

11. What are the two types of checking account fees that banks charge?

_____

_____

_____

Critical Thinking

12. Why is it important to keep your check register up to date?

_____

_____

13. Why do many banks refuse to cash third-party checks?

_____

_____

14. Why should you investigate the fees charged by competing banks before opening your account?

_____

_____

_____

Consumer Applications

15. Sean has a checking account with a monthly maintenance fee of $5.00. The account allows him to write up to eight free checks. For each additional check, he is charged a $0.20 fee. Last month he wrote 15 checks. What was his total fee?

_____

_____

Chapter 7   Banking Services—Where to Stash Your Cash

7.3 Electronic Banking

Key Terms Review

Define each of the following vocabulary terms.

1. electronic funds transfer (EFT) _____

2. automated teller machine (ATM) _____

   _____

3. personal identification number (PIN) _____

   _____

4. direct deposit _____

   _____

5. debit cards _____

   _____

6. automatic withdrawal _____

   _____

Concepts Review

7. What are the advantages of electronic funds transfer?

   _____

   _____

8. Why do you need a PIN to use an ATM?

   _____

   _____

9. How do debit cards work and what are their advantages?

_____

_____

_____

10. How does the Electronic Funds Transfer Act protect consumers?

_____

_____

_____

Critical Thinking

11. What do you think the advantages are of using an ATM?

_____

_____

12. Why do many employees choose to have their paychecks directly deposited into their accounts?

_____

_____

_____

Consumer Applications

13. Kuniko is comparing banks before she opens an account. Mammoth Bank has several branches that are open during evenings and weekends; the bank does not have an ATM nor does it accept direct deposits. First National Bank is only open during the week from 9 A.M. to 3 P.M., but has an extensive network of ATMs, accepts direct deposits, and offers online banking services. Mammoth Bank offers free checking and First National's checking account fee is $5.00 per month. Which bank would you advise Kuniko to use? Why?

_____

_____

_____

Chapter 7   Banking Services—Where To Stash Your Cash

7.4 Balance Your Checkbook

Key Terms Review

Define each of the following vocabulary terms

1. canceled checks_____

Concepts Review

2. What does your bank statement show?

_____

3. How does the account reconciliation form help you?

_____

4. What does it mean if the account is balanced?

_____

5. What should you do if there is an error on your statement?

_____

_____

_____

Critical Thinking

6. What should you do if you cannot reconcile your account?

_____

_____

_____

_____

7. Can you think of reasons why you might need to refer to canceled checks, statements, or reconciliation forms at a later time?

_____

_____

Consumer Applications

8. Aaron received his bank statement with the following information:

Balance Last Statement	Total Deposits	Total Payments	Bank Fees	Balance This Statement
$29.62	$1852.36	$84.03	$6.50	$1791.45

Check No.	Amount	Date		Deposit Amount	Date
123	$43.00	4/2		$987.65	3/31
124	$23.37	4/5		$864.71	4/8
125	$17.66	4/6			

Use the checkbook register form to record each of these transactions.

Number	Date	Description of Transaction	Payment/ Debit (-)	Fee (-)	Deposit/ Credit (+)	BALANCE	

Chapter 7   Banking Services—Where To Stash Your Cash

7.5 Other Banking Services

Key Terms Review

Define each of the following vocabulary terms.

1. certified check_____

_____

_____

2. cashier's check_____

_____

3. money order_____

_____

4. traveler's checks_____

_____

5. wire transfer_____

_____

6. safe deposit boxes_____

Concepts Review

7. What types of purchases are more likely to require a certified or cashier's check?

_____

_____

8. What is the advantage of using a money order rather than a personal check?

_____

_____

9. What are some of the reasons that wire transfers are used?

_____

_____

_____

10. What types of items are usually kept in safe deposit boxes?

_____

_____

Critical Thinking

11. Why do you think banks charge a fee to issue cashier's and certified checks?

_____

_____

12. Why might you use traveler's checks instead of a credit card when you are traveling?

_____

_____

_____

_____

Consumer Applications

13. Clarise was selling her car through a classified advertisement in the paper. When the buyer offered her a personal check, she wasn't sure whether or not to accept it. What would you tell Clarise to do?

_____

_____

_____

_____

_____

Chapter 8   Saving—Plan For Financial Security

8.1 Why Save?

Key Terms Review

Define each of the following vocabulary terms.

1. saving_____

_____

Concepts Review

2. What are some of the reasons to save?

_____

_____

_____

3. How can savings give you flexibility?

_____

_____

_____

4. Why is rewarding yourself an effective saving strategy?

_____

_____

_____

5. How do automatic payroll deductions help you save?

_____

_____

_____

6. What is a checking account transfer and how does it help you save?

_____

_____

_____

_____

Critical Thinking

7. Why do you have a better chance of achieving your saving goals if you start saving when you are young?

_____

_____

_____

8. Why is it important to have a savings strategy?

_____

_____

Consumer Applications

9. Olivia has a part-time job babysitting for two different families. Her hours vary from week to week and so does her income. Her best friend is studying in Australia for the next two semesters, and Olivia would like to save enough money for a plane ticket to visit her. What do you think are the best saving strategies for Olivia to achieve her goal?

_____

_____

_____

_____

_____

_____

Chapter 8   Saving—Plan For Financial Security

8.2 Savings Institutions and Accounts

Key Terms Review

Define each of the following vocabulary terms.

1. commercial bank_____

   _____

2. savings banks_____

3. dividend_____

4. savings and loan associations_____

   _____

5. credit unions_____

   _____

   _____

6. savings accounts_____

   _____

   _____

Concepts Review

7. What type of financial institution is the primary source of loans for businesses?

   _____

8. How are savings and loan associations different from commercial banks?

   _____

   _____

   _____

9. Which are the federal agencies that protect deposits in savings institutions?

_____

_____

_____

_____

10. What factors should you consider in selecting a savings account?

_____

Critical Thinking

11. Why do you think credit unions are able to offer higher interest rates for depositors and low rates for loans?

_____

_____

12. If you had more than $100,000 in a savings account, how could you protect it?

_____

_____

_____

Consumer Applications

13. Ileana has just started teaching at the high school. She currently uses a large commercial bank for her savings. She also has a checking account, a safe deposit box, and a car loan with that bank and has been happy with the service she has received. She now has an opportunity to join the school's credit union. Do you think Ileana should join the credit union? Why or why not?

_____

_____

_____

_____

Chapter 8   Saving—Plan For Financial Security

8.3 Save with Safety

Key Terms Review

Define each of the following vocabulary terms.

1. certificate of deposit (CD)_____

    _____

2. money market account_____

3. annual percentage yield (APY)_____

4. bond_____

5. savings bonds_____

6. face value_____

Concepts Review

7. Why do banks pay lower interest rates on savings accounts than on certificates of deposit?

    _____

    _____

    _____

    _____

8. How do money market accounts differ from regular savings accounts?

    _____

    _____

    _____

    _____

    _____

9. What are the three types of savings bonds? How are they different?

_____

_____

_____

_____

_____

_____

Critical Thinking

10. What are the factors you need to consider when selecting a term for your CD?

_____

_____

_____

_____

11. Why do you think a tax advantage exists on government bonds?

_____

_____

_____

_____

Consumer Applications

12. Maurice's grandmother gave him $500 for high school graduation. He would like to use the money in September for college. If he deposits it in a three-month CD that has an APY of 5.3 percent, how much will he have when the CD matures?

_____

_____

_____

Chapter 8   Saving—Plan For Financial Security

8.4 Simple and Compound Interest

Key Terms Review

Define each of the following vocabulary terms.

1. principal_____

2. simple interest_____

    _____

3. compound interest_____

    _____

Concepts Review

4. Why does the way your bank calculates interest affect how fast your savings grows?

    _____

    _____

    _____

5. What are the ways that interest can be compounded?

    _____

    _____

6. What are the key elements of a successful saving plan?

    _____

7. What are two ways to calculate compound interest?

    _____

8. What is the easiest way to compare account rates offered by different banks?

    _____

Critical Thinking

9. Interest rates on savings accounts are far lower than those with other savings options. Why do you think that the way interest is compounded on savings accounts is of such interest to consumers?

_____

_____

_____

_____

_____

10. Do you think that banks can make mistakes when calculating the interest on your account? Why or why not?

_____

_____

_____

_____

_____

Consumer Applications

11. Vanh has $1,200 to deposit into a savings account. The Annual Percentage Yield is 6 percent. Calculate his balance at the end of one year if the interest is compounded (a) quarterly, (b) semiannually, (c) daily.

_____

_____

_____

_____

_____

_____

_____

Chapter 9   Investing—Prepare For Your Future

9.1 Investing Basics

Key Terms Review

Define each of the following vocabulary terms.

1. investing _____

2. risk _____

3. return _____

4. diversification _____

Concepts Review

5. What is the trade-off to make more income on your investments?

   _____

6. How is the rate of return measured?

   _____

   _____

7. How do age and financial situation affect how you make investment decisions?

   _____

   _____

   _____

   _____

8. How does diversification help limit risk?

   _____

   _____

   _____

9. How does your tolerance for risk affect your choice of investments?

_____

_____

_____

Critical Thinking

10. Why is it important to invest in ways that are consistent with your values? What are some of the values that you have that would affect your investments?

_____

_____

_____

_____

11. Do you think a higher rate of return is worth the risk of losing your investment? Explain your answer.

_____

_____

_____

_____

_____

Consumer Applications

12. Monique bought 300 shares of stock for $31.25 per share. The corporation paid a $0.50 per share dividend last year. After one year, she sold the stock for $33.75 per share. What was the total amount of her return on this investment? What was her rate of return?

_____

_____

_____

_____

Chapter 9   Investing—Prepare For Your Future

9.2 How to Invest in Corporations

Key Terms Review

Define each of the following vocabulary terms.

1. share of stock_____

2. stockholders_____

    _____

3. dividend_____

4. transactions_____

5. stockbroker_____

    _____

6. brokerage firm_____

    _____

7. stock exchange_____

8. National Association of Securities Dealers Automated Quotation System_____

    _____

9. capital gain_____

10. capital loss_____

    _____

11. preferred stock_____

12. common stock_____

13. blue chip stocks_____

14. growth stock_____

15. high-yield bonds_____

16. Why do stock prices change?

_____

_____

_____

17. What is the difference between buying stock in a corporation and buying its bonds?

_____

_____

Critical Thinking

18. Selling stock and corporate bonds are two ways for a corporation to raise money for the business. How do you think corporations decide whether to sell stock or bonds?

_____

_____

_____

_____

_____

Consumer Applications

19. Tula is 24 years old. She is investing in X Corporation as part of her retirement plan. X Corporation is a blue-chip stock; both preferred and common stock are offered. Which type of stock would you advise Tula to buy and why?

_____

_____

_____

_____

_____

Chapter 9   Investing—Prepare For Your Future

9.3 How to Invest in Mutual Funds

Key Terms Review

Define each of the following vocabulary terms.

1. mutual fund_____

    _____

2. load_____

Concepts Review

3. What are some of the reasons for choosing to invest in mutual funds?

    _____

    _____

    _____

4. What are the costs associated with mutual funds?

    _____

    _____

5. What is the difference between a front-end load fund and a back-end load fund?

    _____

    _____

6. What are the four categories of mutual fund investment objectives? For each category, list where it fits in on the risk/return pyramid.

    _____

    _____

    _____

7. Besides risk/return objectives, list and describe other common investment objectives of mutual funds.

    _____

    _____

    _____

    _____

    _____

Critical Thinking

8. Why do you think some mutual funds are no-load funds? Do you think that they are as profitable as funds that have a load?

    _____

    _____

    _____

    _____

9. According to *The Wall Street Journal*, there are more mutual funds than individual stocks traded on the New York Stock Exchange? Why do you think mutual funds have become such a popular investment?

    _____

    _____

Consumer Applications

10. Harris' aunt gave him $5,000 to help him start saving for a house. In what mutual fund categories would you recommend he invest and why?

    _____

    _____

    _____

    _____

    _____

Chapter 9   Investing—Prepare For Your Future

9.4 Research Investments

Key Terms Review

Define each of the following vocabulary terms.

1. prospectus _____

   _____

2. Securities Exchange Commission (SEC) _____

   _____

3. insider trading _____

   _____

Concepts Review

4. List some of the printed sources of information on stocks, bonds, and mutual funds. What type of information do they provide?

   _____

   _____

   _____

   _____

   _____

   _____

5. How can the Internet help you with your investments?

   _____

   _____

   _____

6. What is the NASD? How does it benefit you?

_____

_____

_____

_____

Critical Thinking

7. What might be some of the reasons you would select a discount broker instead of a full service broker?

_____

_____

_____

_____

8. What information in a stock quote will help you decide whether or not to invest?

_____

_____

_____

_____

Consumer Applications

9. Ramona sells electronic testers to manufacturers. One of her customers has just made a very large purchase and has indicated that the company will be purchasing more in the future because it is buying a competing manufacturer. Ramona is certain of the identity of the company they are buying. Should she invest in that company before the purchase is made? Why or why not?

_____

_____

_____

Chapter 9   Investing—Prepare For Your Future

9.5 Retirement and Other Investments

Key Terms Review

Define each of the following vocabulary terms.

1. 401(k) plan_____

2. individual retirement account (IRA)_____

_____

Concepts Review

3. What are the main benefits of retirement plans?

_____

_____

_____

4. Why is a 401(k) plan an excellent way to save for retirement?

_____

_____

_____

_____

5. Why might you invest in an IRA rather than a 401(k) plan?

_____

6. What are the advantages and disadvantages of investment clubs?

_____

_____

_____

_____

7. How can you earn returns on collected items? Is this a good form of investing?

_____

_____

_____

_____

Critical Thinking

8. Why do you think many companies have discontinued offering pension plans for their employees and now offer 401(k) plans instead?

_____

_____

_____

9. How might you protect yourself from loss when investing in real estate?

_____

_____

_____

_____

Consumer Applications

10. Rashawn has just graduated from college and accepted a job. The company offers a 401(k) plan. Rashawn is nervous about his ability to pay for his apartment and his car and cannot decide whether to invest in the plan now or to wait until his financial situation improves. What advice would you give him?

_____

_____

_____

_____

Chapter 10   Credit—You're in Charge

10.1 What Is Credit?

Key Terms Review

Define each of the following vocabulary terms.

1. credit_____

Concepts Review

2. What trade-off do you make when you use credit?

   _____

3. When is borrowing almost a necessity?

   _____

4. What is equity?

   _____

   _____

5. Why is home ownership sometimes an investment?

   _____

   _____

6. Other than as an investment, what is another good reason to own a home?

   _____

7. Why is education sometimes an investment?

   _____

   _____

8. What maximum percentage of your take-home pay should go for debt payment?

   _____

Critical Thinking

9. Why do you think banks, credit card companies, and other lending institutions put a maximum on how much someone can borrow?

_____

_____

_____

10. How do you think the businesses mentioned in Exercise 9 determine the maximum amount a person can borrow?

_____

_____

_____

Consumer Applications

11. Salvador and Aurelia are borrowing $150,000 to buy a new house. They must decide whether to borrow the money for 15 years at 8 percent interest, or 30 years at 8 1/2 percent interest. If they choose the 15-year mortgage, their monthly payments would be $9.56 per $1,000 borrowed, or $1,434. If they choose the 30-year mortgage, their monthly payments would be $7.69 per $1,000 borrowed, or $1,153.50. How much more money would they have to spend each month if they choose the 15-year mortgage? How much would they be paying for the house if they take out a 15-year mortgage? 30-year mortgage? What is the total difference?

_____

_____

_____

_____

_____

Chapter 10   Credit—You're in Charge

10.2 How to Qualify for Credit

Key Terms Review

Define each of the following vocabulary terms.

1. creditworthiness_____

2. character_____

3. credit history_____

4. cosign (a loan)_____

5. capacity_____

6. capital_____

7. credit bureau_____

    _____

8. credit rating_____

Concepts Review

9. What are the three factors that lenders use to judge creditworthiness?

    _____

10. What is always the most important factor in being able to get credit in the future?

    _____

11. If you have no credit history, what are some other signs of responsibility that a lender may consider?

    _____

    _____

12. What information can hurt your credit rating?

    _____

13. What information can help your credit rating?

_____

_____

Critical Thinking

14. Your best friend, whom you've known for more than ten years, has asked you to cosign a loan for her to buy a car because she can't get a loan on her own. On what would you base your decision?

_____

_____

_____

15. Why do you think lenders want to know your credit history and current financial obligations before they decide to lend you more money?

_____

_____

_____

Consumer Applications

16. Ruben has never had a problem getting a loan. He has a motorcycle, a car and two major credit cards. Now, he found another car, a two-seater convertible sports car, that he really wants to buy. When he went to apply for the loan, he was denied. What should Ruben do to find out why he was denied? Why do you think he was denied? What decision would you make if you were Ruben?

_____

_____

_____

_____

_____

Chapter 10   Credit—You're in Charge

10.3 Sources of Consumer Credit

Key Terms Review

Define each of the following vocabulary terms.

1. secured loan_____

2. collateral_____

3. installment loan_____

_____

4. unsecured loan_____

5. regular charge account_____

_____

6. revolving charge account_____

_____

7. grace period_____

_____

8. credit limit_____

Concepts Review

9. What is the difference between a secured loan and an unsecured loan?

_____

_____

10. Is a credit card considered a secured loan or an unsecured loan?

_____

11. How do savings and loan associations differ from banks and credit unions?

_____

_____

_____

12. What are other sources of consumer loans?

_____

_____

Critical Thinking

13. Why do you think interest rates on credit cards are higher than almost any other type of consumer credit?

_____

_____

_____

_____

14. If you were issued a credit card, you might be tempted to charge many items that you otherwise might not buy. How could you make sure that you would be careful and not get too heavily into debt?

_____

_____

Consumer Applications

15. For the first 10 days in a 30-day month, Yuan's balance on his credit card was $200. He then made a payment of $150, bringing his balance down to $50 for the remaining 20 days. What was Yuan's average daily balance? If his interest rate is 12 percent a year, what would the interest rate be for one month? Multiply the average daily balance by the monthly interest rate to get Yuan's finance charge for that month. [Average Daily Balance = Sum of Daily Balances ÷ Number of Days.]

_____

_____

Chapter 10   Credit—You're in Charge

10.4 Credit Rights and Responsibilities

Key Terms Review

Define each of the following vocabulary terms.

1. Truth-in-Lending Act _____

_____

2. finance charge _____

3. annual percentage rate (APR) _____

_____

4. Equal Credit Opportunity Act _____

_____

5. Fair Credit Reporting Act _____

6. Consumer Credit Reporting Reform Act _____

_____

7. Fair Credit Billing Act _____

_____

8. Fair Debt Collections Practices Act _____

_____

Concepts Review

Circle the answer that best describes the statement in the exercises that follow:

9. True / False   The law requires the credit bureau to investigate disputed items on a credit report within 30 days.

10. True / False   It is fair to assume that the credit bureau will take care of a problem for you.

11. True / False   If you believe a charge on your credit card statement is wrong, you can simply ignore that bill and deduct it from the amount you owe.

12. True / False   If you believe a product you bought with a credit card is of inferior quality, you must first try to settle the problem with the merchant who sold you the merchandise.

13. True / False   A lender will always limit your credit because it is trying to protect you from financial difficulties.

_____

Critical Thinking

14. Why would you care if the information on your credit report is accurate?

_____

_____

_____

15. Why must you write to your credit card company as opposed to calling when you have a disputed bill?

_____

_____

_____

Consumer Applications

16. Lyndsay took her car to the mechanic to get her air-conditioner repaired. The bill was $600, and she put it on one of her major credit cards. Several days later, her air-conditioner stopped working. Her mechanic told her it would cost another $400 to repair it. Lyndsay wanted her mechanic to refund her the original $600, as she got nothing for her money. Her mechanic refused. What action should Lyndsay take?

_____

_____

_____

_____

Chapter 10   Credit—You're in Charge

10.5 Maintain a Good Credit Rating

Key Terms Review

Define each of the following vocabulary terms.

1. acceleration clause_____

_____

2. balloon payment_____

_____

3. bankruptcy_____

_____

4. true-name fraud_____

_____

5. debt consolidation loan_____

_____

Concepts Review

6. If you would like to establish credit, how would you build a positive record?

_____

_____

_____

7. How can both a husband and wife establish credit in his/her own name?

_____

_____

_____

8. How can you avoid some common credit problems?

_____

_____

9. What is the best way to protect yourself from true-name fraud?

_____

_____

Critical Thinking

10. Why are debt-consolidation loans a "bandage, not a cure"?

_____

_____

_____

_____

11. What happens to a car's value over time? If you didn't pay very much toward the loan on your car at the beginning, and then had a balloon payment at the end, how could your car's value compare with the balance of the loan?

_____

_____

_____

Consumer Applications

12. Maria received a phone call from "Dream Vacations, Inc." She was told that she was selected to receive an all-expenses-paid, four-day vacation to Disney World. The representative asked for information such as her full name and address, which Maria gave her. Then the woman said she needed a security deposit to hold Maria's reservation at the hotel. She asked Maria for her social security number and a major credit card number. Should Maria give her the information? Why or why not? What else should Maria do?

_____

_____

_____

Chapter 11   Budget Essentials—Food, Clothes, and Fun

11.1 Nutrition Facts

Key Terms Review

Define each of the following vocabulary terms.

1. nutrients_____

2. calories_____

3. carbohydrates_____

4. fiber_____

   _____

5. proteins_____

6. fats_____

   _____

7. cholesterol_____

8. vitamins_____

9. minerals_____

10. balanced diet_____

11. Food Guide Pyramid_____

    _____

12. serving_____

13. anorexia_____

    _____

14. bulimia_____

15. obesity_____

Concepts Review

16. What are the six basic nutrients that help your body run?

_____

17. How can you use the Food Guide Pyramid to make healthy food choices?

_____

_____

18. What are the dangers of obesity?

_____

_____

Critical Thinking

19. Why is a breakfast comprised of mostly carbohydrates not ideal?

_____

_____

20. Why would a life insurance company be concerned with your weight and overall health?

_____

_____

Consumer Applications

21. Enrique knows that proteins are essential for building and repairing cells, as well as supplying energy. He wants to gain weight and build muscle, so he puts himself on a high-protein diet, consisting of a lot of meat, fish, and eggs. What is the danger of this kind of diet? What should Enrique eat in order to accomplish his goal?

_____

_____

_____

_____

Chapter 11   Budget Essentials—Food, Clothes, and Fun

11.2 Shop for a Healthful Diet

Key Terms Review

Define each of the following vocabulary terms.

1. daily values_____

2. expiration date_____

3. unit price_____

Concepts Review

4. How can you best go about shopping within your budget?

    _____

    _____

    _____

    _____

5. What are two reasons why you should bring a shopping list?

    _____

    _____

    _____

    _____

6. How does unit pricing make shopping easier?

    _____

    _____

    _____

    _____

Critical Thinking

7. How do laws governing claims on packaged foods protect consumers?

_____

_____

_____

_____

8. Why would a consumer need to read the Nutrition Facts of any product?

_____

_____

_____

9. Why are the more profitable products placed at eye level where the consumer would look first?

_____

_____

_____

Consumer Applications

10. Fatima is on a low-fat, low-sodium diet. She must decide which breakfast bar to buy:

    Breakfast Bar #1   Breakfast Bar #2

    Total fat 1 g   Total fat 4 g

    Sodium 210 mg   Sodium 70 mg

    Which one should she buy?

_____

_____

_____

_____

Chapter 11   Budget Essentials—Food, Clothes, and Fun

11.3 Evaluate Clothes Choices

Key Terms Review

Define each of the following vocabulary terms.

1. utility_____

2. style_____

3. fads_____

4. classics_____

5. designer clothes_____

6. natural fibers_____

7. manufactured fibers_____

Concepts Review

8. What three benefits do you consider when making a clothing purchase?

    _____

9. What are the advantages and disadvantages of cotton?

    _____

    _____

10. For what time of year is linen good and why?

    _____

11. For what time of year is wool good and why?

    _____

    _____

    _____

Critical Thinking

12. Why do most people have few silk garments in their wardrobes?

_____

_____

_____

_____

13. What are advantages and disadvantages of buying clothes from a catalog (either printed or on the Internet)?

_____

_____

_____

_____

14. Why do you think laws were passed requiring content and care labels in all clothing sold in the United States?

_____

_____

Consumer Applications

15. Paul took a summer job with the Parks Department mowing and raking local parks. He needs to buy some sturdy clothes for his job but can't decide between the no-name jeans for $35 a pair and designer jeans for $50 a pair. Because he'll have to wash the jeans each day he wears them, he would like to get five pairs. Also, at the end of the summer, he wouldn't wear the no-name jeans to school but would wear designer jeans. How much would each option cost him? How much would he save by buying the no-name brand? Which option would you choose?

_____

_____

_____

_____

Chapter 11   Budget Essentials—Food, Clothes, and Fun

11.4 Recreation and Travel

Key Terms Review

Define each of the following vocabulary terms.

1. standby_____

_____

Concepts Review

2. How can you measure the value of money?

_____

3. If you have many interests and are trying to decide what recreational activities you would like to pursue, what do you need to consider in addition to your budget?

_____

_____

4. When and where can you find the best prices on sports equipment and clothing?

_____

_____

5. When you're comparing prices of equipment, what should you consider?

_____

_____

6. If you wanted to go on vacation, what sources would be available to help you decide where to go? What information would you need?

_____

_____

_____

Critical Thinking

7. If you wanted to buy some equipment, either for exercise or recreation, and were not knowledgeable and on a budget, where would you go first, a sporting goods store or a discount store?

_____

_____

_____

_____

8. If you take public transportation to your destination, what is a big disadvantage when considering your budget?

_____

_____

_____

9. Rooms in chain hotels or motels typically are the same wherever you go and local hotels or motels may be more interesting. Why might you choose a chain over a local hotel or motel?

_____

_____

_____

Consumer Applications

10. Sarah's new boyfriend is an avid skier, and she decided that she would like to try it, too. To ski, she needs equipment and clothing. Should she go out and buy it all at once?

_____

_____

_____

_____

_____

Chapter 12   Transportation—How Will You Get There?

12.1 Transportation Basics

Concepts Review

1. What are some of the ways the government monitors transportation conditions?

   _____

   _____

2. What are some transportation options besides a car?

   _____

   _____

3. What things must you consider before shopping for a bicycle?

   _____

   _____

4. What are some sources of information about bicycles?

   _____

   _____

5. What trade-offs do you need to make when shopping for a motorcycle?

   _____

   _____

6. What type of safety equipment should you wear when using bicycles, in-line skates, or motorcycles?

   _____

   _____

   _____

7. How can using public transportation help the environment?

_____

_____

8. What are the benefits of carpooling?

_____

_____

Critical Thinking

9. Why do you think in-line skates are such a popular form of transportation?

_____

_____

10. Why are motorcycles expensive to insure?

_____

_____

11. Public transportation has many benefits. Why do you think that many people with access to public transportation do not use it and drive their cars instead?

_____

_____

_____

_____

Consumer Applications

12. Maxine has accepted a job at a nursing home after school. The nursing home is one mile from the high school. There are bus stops within one block of the high school, the nursing home, and Maxine's house. Maxine is hoping that she can save enough money from her job to buy a car. Do you think this is an appropriate goal for Maxine? Why or why not?

_____

_____

_____

Chapter 12   Transportation—How Will You Get There?

12.2 How to Choose a Car

Key Terms Review

Define each of the following vocabulary terms.

1. odometer_____

2. features_____

3. options_____

Concepts Review

4. What are some of the costs of owning a car?

   _____

5. How do you determine whether or not you can afford a car?

   _____

   _____

   _____

   _____

6. What are the advantages of owning a new car?

   _____

7. How do you determine what class of vehicle to buy?

   _____

8. How can printed information help you decide which car to buy?

   _____

   _____

   _____

9. What features may contribute to a car's safety?

_____

10. Why do you need to carefully inspect a used car before buying?

_____

_____

Critical Thinking

11. What are the advantages and disadvantages of buying a used car from a dealer? From an individual?

_____

_____

_____

12. For several hundred dollars, most dealers offer a warranty extension on a new car. Do you think this is a worthwhile purchase? Why or why not?

_____

_____

_____

_____

Consumer Applications

13. Amelia wants to buy a $15,000 car. She has $4,000 for a down payment. Her bank told her that the monthly loan payment would be $298. Her weekly take-home pay is $750 per week. Her monthly expenses are as follows. Can she afford to buy this car? (There are four weeks per month.)

Rent: $1,350   Entertainment: $100

Food: $400   Car insurance: $100

Phone: $40   Gas & maintenance: $50

Utilities: $60   Savings: $200

_____

_____

Chapter 12   Transportation—How Will You Get There?

12.3 To Buy or Lease?

Key Terms Review

Define each of the following vocabulary terms.

1. rebate_____

2. leasing_____

_____

Concepts Review

3. Why has leasing automobiles become popular?

_____

_____

4. What is the gross capitalized cost of a lease? Why is it important?

_____

_____

5. How does the number of miles you drive affect your lease payment?

_____

_____

_____

_____

6. When should a person consider leasing a vehicle rather than buying it?

_____

_____

_____

7. What are some of the insurance policies offered by the Finance and Insurance (F&I) manager and how do they protect you?

_____

_____

_____

_____

8. What information is contained in the car sales contract?

_____

_____

Critical Thinking

9. What do you think are the advantages of buying the car you have leased?

_____

_____

_____

10. Why do dealers offer either a rebate or a low interest rate, but not both?

_____

_____

_____

Consumer Applications

11. Chi-luan is negotiating the price of a car with a salesperson. The salesperson has not disclosed the price of the car Chi-luan wants but has asked him how much he can afford to pay for a monthly payment. Should Chi-luan give the salesperson this information? Why or why not?

_____

_____

_____

Chapter 12   Transportation—How Will You Get There?

12.4 The Car-Buying Process

Key Terms Review

Define each of the following vocabulary terms.

1. invoice price _____

2. sticker price _____

_____

Concepts Review

3. Why do you need to know the invoice price to negotiate a price with a dealer?

_____

_____

4. How can you determine the value of your trade-in?

_____

_____

5. How do you decide from which dealer to buy?

_____

_____

6. What are the advantages and disadvantages of no-haggle dealers?

_____

_____

7. Why are certain times of the month or year better to buy a car than others?

_____

_____

_____

_____

_____

8. Why should you negotiate the value of your trade-in separately, after you have already agreed on the price of the new car?

_____

_____

9. What are some of the additional charges you can expect to pay after you settle on a price?

_____

Critical Thinking

10. Why will you get the best price for your car by selling it yourself rather than trading it in?

_____

_____

11. Why do you think the MSRP is displayed in the window rather than the actual price the dealer expects consumers to pay?

_____

_____

_____

Consumer Applications

12. Latisha has decided to buy a new minivan. She researched the invoice price for the model she wants and determined that it is $26,000. She is adding three options: alloy wheels (invoice $200), leather seats (invoice $800), and a roof rack (invoice $100). The manufacturer's rebate is $1,500. What is a fair price that she should seek in negotiating with the dealer?

_____

_____

_____

Chapter 12   Transportation—How Will You Get There?

12.5 How to Maintain a Car

Key Terms Review

Define each of the following vocabulary terms.

1. owner's manual _____

2. maintenance schedule _____

3. rebuilt or reconditioned _____

   _____

4. lemon laws _____

Concepts Review

5. What type of information is contained in the owner's manual?

   _____

   _____

   _____

6. Why is it important to follow the maintenance schedule?

   _____

   _____

7. Why is it important to check your tires on a regular basis?

   _____

   _____

8. Why is maintaining your oil an important part of car maintenance?

   _____

   _____

9. What is the best way to locate a reputable repair shop for your car?

_____

_____

10. What is the best way to resolve problems with a repair shop?

_____

_____

_____

Critical Thinking

11. Why do dealerships charge more for repairs than independent shops? Why would you bring your car to the dealer to be repaired?

_____

_____

_____

12. Why do you think the law requires that repair shops return your old parts if you request them?

_____

_____

Consumer Applications

13. Kirsten took her car to the repair shop because it was making a lot of noise and she thought she might need a new muffler. She received and signed a written price estimate for the repair. When she returned to the shop to get her car, the technician told her that the entire exhaust system needed to be replaced and that he had completed the work. The charge for the service was substantially more than the written estimate. What should Kirsten do?

_____

_____

_____

Chapter 13   Housing—A Place to Call Home

13.1 Your Housing Options

Key Terms Review

Define each of the following vocabulary terms.

1. dormitories_____

_____

2. efficiency apartment_____

_____

3. duplex apartment_____

4. condominium_____

5. mobile home_____

_____

6. lease_____

_____

_____

Concepts Review

7. If you want to rent an apartment and don't have enough furniture or money to buy furniture, what are your options?

_____

_____

8. What facilities might you find at an apartment complex?

_____

_____

9. When you own a condominium (or townhouse), what do your "condo association fees" pay for?

_____

_____

10. Of your ownership options (house, condominium, mobile home), which one does not increase in value over time?

_____

Critical Thinking

11. Why do you think most colleges and universities require their freshmen students to live on campus?

_____

_____

_____

12. Why is it important to discuss rules of behavior and division of responsibilities with a prospective roommate before you move in together and/or sign a lease?

_____

_____

_____

Consumer Applications

13. Deanna and Sharon are considering moving in together into a two-bedroom apartment. They are both nurses. Deanna works from 7:00 a.m. to 3:30 p.m., and Sharon works from 3:00 p.m. to 11:30 p.m. They feel that this is ideal, because they won't be home together very often, and they'll both have the place to themselves a large part of the time. Do you think they still need to agree on rules of behavior and division of responsibilities?

_____

_____

_____

_____

Chapter 13 Housing—A Place to Call Home

13.2 How to Rent an Apartment

Key Terms Review

Define each of the following vocabulary terms.

1. tenant_____

2. landlord_____

3. security deposit_____

_____

Concepts Review

4. How do you start your search for an apartment?

_____

5. How do you know how much rent you can afford?

_____

6. What are some sources of finding an apartment?

_____

7. What is the purpose of a checklist?

_____

_____

8. What is the purpose of a lease?

_____

_____

9. Why do you think landlords disallow or require an extra security deposit for waterbeds?

_____

_____

_____

_____

_____

10. What would you ask the current tenants and neighbors of an apartment that you were interested in renting?

_____

_____

_____

_____

Consumer Applications

11. Deanna and Sharon stayed in their apartment together for two years and can now afford to move out into a bigger one with more amenities. Prior to moving in, they walked through the apartment with the landlord and made a list of any existing damage. Now, they are getting ready to move. What would you recommend to them to make sure they get their security deposit back?

_____

_____

_____

_____

_____

_____

Chapter 13   Housing—A Place to Call Home

13.3 How to Buy a Home

Key Terms Review

Define each of the following vocabulary terms.

1. mortgage _____

2. principal _____

3. points _____

_____

4. closing costs _____

5. escrow account _____

_____

6. mortgage insurance _____

_____

7. fixed-rate mortgage _____

8. adjustable-rate mortgages (ARMs) _____

_____

9. FHA mortgage _____

_____

10. VA mortgage _____

_____

11. graduated-payment mortgage _____

12. appreciates _____

13. home equity loan _____

_____

14. offer _____

15. earnest money _____

Concepts Review

16. What is the greatest advantage of a fixed-rate mortgage?

_____

17. What percent of your income can you generally afford when you're buying a house?

_____

Critical Thinking

18. Why do you think lenders require homeowners to carry homeowner's insurance?

_____

_____

19. Why do you think lenders require an escrow account to be set up?

_____

Consumer Applications

20. Ed and Elaine are buying their first house and have saved $20,000 for a down payment on a $100,000 house. They are eligible for an FHA loan that would require them to put only $10,000 down. If they go with a conventional 30-year mortgage at 8 percent interest, they would have to pay $7.34 per month for each $1,000 they borrow. If they choose the FHA mortgage, their interest rate will be 7.5 percent, and they will have to pay only $7.00 per month for each $1,000 they borrow. What would their monthly payments be with either loan if you disregard escrow payments for taxes and insurance? Which loan should they choose?

_____

_____

_____

_____

Chapter 13   Housing—A Place to Call Home

13.4 How to Furnish Your Home

Concepts Review

1. How can you plan what you need when you are starting to furnish your home?

    _____

    _____

2. What are three considerations involved when choosing what furniture to buy?

    _____

    _____

3. When shopping for furniture and appliances, should you buy the highest-quality or the lowest-priced item?

    _____

    _____

    _____

    _____

    _____

    _____

4. What type of wood makes the highest quality furniture? Why?

    _____

    _____

    _____

5. What is an *appliance*?

    _____

    _____

6. What is one good way to find out about the strengths and weaknesses of different brands?

_____

7. Of what things should you be sure when you buy a floor model of an appliance?

_____

Critical Thinking

8. Your textbook gives two examples of appliances that are necessities, a furnace and a water heater. List two more appliances that are necessities, and then list ten appliances that are luxuries. How many of these luxuries are in your home?

_____

_____

_____

9. If you were looking at two different appliances that were the same price, but one had more options than the other, what might that tell you about the quality of each of the appliances?

_____

_____

_____

Consumer Applications

10. When Patti and Steve bought their home, they wanted to upgrade their major kitchen appliances and furnish their living room. Patti wanted a new refrigerator and dishwasher. Steve wanted a new couch and TV so they could put the old TV in their bedroom. What would you say would be a fair solution if they could only afford two new items?

_____

_____

_____

_____

Chapter 14   Automobile and Home Insurance—Sharing the Risk

14.1 Insurance Basics

Key Terms Review

Define each of the following vocabulary terms.

1. insurance_____

_____

2. premium_____

3. policy_____

4. claim_____

5. shared risk_____

_____

6. insurable interest_____

7. appraisal_____

8. rider_____

9. property insurance_____

_____

10. market value_____

11. replacement value_____

_____

12. liability insurance_____

Concepts Review

13. What is risk management?

_____

14. How do insurance companies use statistics?

_____

_____

_____

_____

15. What is the difference between market value and replacement value?

_____

_____

Critical Thinking

16. How do you think you can determine the amount of life insurance to buy?

_____

_____

17. Do you think it costs more to insure something for market value or replacement value? Explain your answer.

_____

_____

_____

Consumer Applications

18. Kendra has two children and is opening a day-care center in her home. She has purchased all of the necessary equipment and has created an outdoor play space. What type of insurance does she need to protect herself and her business?

_____

_____

_____

_____

Chapter 14 Automobile and Home Insurance—Sharing the Risk

14.2 Automobile Insurance

Key Terms Review

Define each of the following vocabulary terms.

1. bodily injury liability coverage_____

_____

2. deductible_____

3. points_____

_____

4. assigned risk_____

_____

Concepts Review

5. How do you interpret the numbers 100/300 on your insurance policy?

_____

_____

_____

6. What does comprehensive insurance cover?

_____

_____

7. How is the cost of collision and comprehensive insurance determined?

_____

_____

8. How does the deductible you choose affect your premium?

_____

_____

9. What are some reasons for increasing insurance costs?

_____

_____

_____

Critical Thinking

10. Insurance companies classify policyholders by age, sex, and marital status, and they charge different premiums depending on the person's classification. Do you think this is discrimination? Explain your answer.

_____

_____

11. Since all states require drivers to purchase insurance, why is it important to also purchase uninsured motorist insurance?

_____

_____

Consumer Applications

12. Ivy was driving in a severe rainstorm and she collided with another car. The two passengers in the other vehicle were injured and filed suit. One claim was for $150,000 and the other was for $175,000. The driver of the other car was not harmed, but his vehicle sustained damage totaling $6,600. Ivy's bodily injury liability coverage is 100/300/50. How much money will Ivy's insurance pay to settle these claims? How much will Ivy be responsible for paying?

_____

_____

_____

_____

Chapter 14 Automobile and Home Insurance—Sharing the Risk

14.3 Home Insurance Coverage

Key Terms Review

Define each of the following vocabulary terms.

1. homeowner's insurance_____

2. umbrella policy_____

_____

3. renter's insurance_____

_____

_____

4. 80 percent rule_____

_____

_____

Concepts Review

5. What are the two types of coverage provided by a homeowner's insurance policy?

_____

6. Which type of coverage do you think would be higher? Why?

_____

_____

_____

7. What are some special risks that ordinary homeowner's insurance does not cover?

_____

_____

8. What are the premiums charged for homeowner's insurance based on? What does this tell the underwriters?

_____

_____

_____

Critical Thinking

9. Why do you think that there are some exclusions in a homeowner's insurance policy? Why would the homeowner have to buy a special rider to cover certain items?

_____

_____

_____

_____

10. Why do you think the owner, not the tenant, is responsible for the homeowner's insurance covering the structure or accidents that take place outside the structure?

_____

_____

_____

_____

Consumer Applications

11. John's family has owned an old Victorian home for several generations. The home has never been upgraded or modernized. John recently inherited the home; he and his wife Nadine moved into the home currently valued at $80,000. What things can they do to decrease their insurance premiums?

_____

_____

_____

_____

Chapter 14   Automobile and Home Insurance—Sharing the Risk

14.4 Providers and the Claims Process

Key Terms Review

Define each of the following vocabulary terms.

1. no-fault insurance_____

_____

Concepts Review

2. What do you expect to get from your insurance in exchange for your premium?

_____

_____

3. Why should you not necessarily buy insurance from a company that offers the lowest price?

_____

_____

_____

4. What is the function of an insurance agent?

_____

5. What are two kinds of insurance agents, and what is the difference?

_____

_____

6. If you wanted to learn about the best insurance companies, and you checked *Best's Insurance Reports*, what information would you find?

_____

_____

_____

7. What is the easiest way to check an insurance company's claim service and what information will it provide?

_____

_____

_____

Critical Thinking

8. In addition to taking pictures of each room, what would be the easiest, safest, and most accurate way to keep track of all your electronic equipment and appliances to determine their value?

_____

_____

_____

9. Why do many insurance companies pay contractors or automobile repair shops directly for claims instead of the insured party? Why would the company care whether the home or car is repaired?

_____

_____

_____

_____

Consumer Applications

10. Meryam was involved in an accident with another driver. It was clearly the other driver's fault, and the driver even admitted it. As they exchanged information, the driver begged Meryam not to report it to the police or file the claim with her insurance company. Because he had a bad driving record, he feared he would lose his license or his insurance company would either raise his rates or drop him. He promised to reimburse her out of his pocket. What should Meryam do?

_____

_____

_____

_____

Chapter 15   Health and Life Insurance—Your Personal Security

15.1 Health Insurance Basics

Key Terms Review

Define each of the following vocabulary terms.

1. malpractice insurance_____

_____

2. generic drugs_____

_____

Concepts Review

3. What are some of the contributing factors to the rising cost of healthcare?

_____

_____

4. What does the hospitalization portion of a policy cover?

_____

_____

_____

5. What additional insurance coverage can you purchase?

_____

6. What are some health needs for which you might need special coverage?

_____

_____

_____

Critical Thinking

7. Why do you think many policies exclude coverage for medications such as diet drugs, experimental drugs, and those that treat cosmetic appearance?

_____

_____

_____

8. Do you think that doctors need more malpractice insurance today than they did 20 years ago? Why or why not?

_____

_____

_____

_____

Consumer Applications

9. Nomar owns a roofing business. He is married, has four children, and owns his own home. One of his children has a hereditary heart condition that needs monthly monitoring at the hospital. What type of insurance coverage do you think Nomar should purchase? Explain your answer.

_____

_____

_____

_____

_____

_____

_____

_____

_____

Chapter 15   Health and Life Insurance—Your Personal Security

15.2 Health Insurance Plans

Key Terms Review

Define each of the following vocabulary terms.

1. fee-for-service plan_____

2. 80/20 coverage_____

   _____

3. coinsurance_____

4. reasonable and customary charges_____

   _____

5. managed care plans_____

   _____

6. capitation_____

   _____

7. copayment_____

   _____

8. health maintenance organization (HMO)_____

   _____

9. primary care physician_____

10. preferred provider organization (PPO)_____

    _____

11. point-of-service (POS) plan_____

    _____

Concepts Review

12. What is the relationship between the amount of deductible you choose and your premium?

_____

13. What are the three basic types of managed care plans?

_____

14. Which managed care plan is most like a fee-for-service plan?

_____

Critical Thinking

15. How do you think insurance companies determine what is a reasonable and customary charge for a particular service?

_____

_____

_____

16. Why do most managed care plans require you to obtain preapproval for nonemergency hospitalization?

_____

_____

Consumer Applications

17. Mitchell's fee-for-service insurance policy has a $300 deductible and 80/20 coverage. He was hospitalized for pneumonia and the charges totaled $2,200. His insurance company's reasonable and customary charge for this treatment is $1,900. How much will Mitchell pay for his treatment? How much will the insurance company pay?

_____

_____

_____

_____

Chapter 15   Health and Life Insurance—Your Personal Security

15.3 Choose a Health Plan

Key Terms Review

Define each of the following vocabulary terms.

1. open enrollment_____

_____

2. COBRA_____

_____

_____

3. pre-existing condition_____

_____

4. Medigap_____

_____

5. Medicaid_____

6. workers' compensation_____

_____

Concepts Review

7. Why are health insurance premiums for groups lower than those for individuals?

_____

_____

8. How can a pre-existing condition affect your insurance coverage?

_____

_____

9. What qualifications do you need to meet to qualify for Medicare? For Medicaid?

_____

_____

10. What should be your goal in buying insurance?

_____

_____

Critical Thinking

11. Why do you think it is necessary to ask yourself so many questions to help determine what health care coverage is most important to you?

_____

_____

12. When you begin your job at a company, why might there be a waiting period to be covered by the new employer's health plan?

_____

_____

_____

_____

Consumer Applications

13. Zachary works part-time. His employer has recently informed him that he will now be eligible for health benefits. Zachary currently has an individual policy. Because of a skin condition, Zachary goes regularly to a dermatologist. This doctor would not be covered under Zachary's new plan. What issues does Zachary face in making the decision to either continue his individual policy or accept the employer's health plan?

_____

_____

_____

_____

Chapter 15   Health and Life Insurance—Your Personal Security

15.4 Health Care Rights and Responsibilities

Key Terms Review

Define each of the following vocabulary terms.

1. patients' bill of rights_____

2. referral_____

_____

Concepts Review

3. Why is it your responsibility to become involved in health care decisions?

_____

_____

4. Why is it your responsibility to report wrongdoing and fraud to authorities, even if it doesn't affect your health or treatment?

_____

_____

5. What is a potential problem with the referral policy of many managed plans?

_____

_____

6. Why do managed care plans require you to choose your doctors from among those who participate in the plan?

_____

_____

_____

7. If you cannot resolve a dispute over an unpaid claim with your insurance company, what should you do?

_____

_____

_____

Critical Thinking

8. Why do you think many insurance companies and providers voluntarily follow the proposed patients' bill of rights?

_____

_____

_____

9. Why might a primary care physician refuse to refer you to a specialist?

_____

_____

_____

Consumer Applications

10. Jonas was diagnosed with a very rare form of cancer. His physicians have told him that regular cancer treatments would be ineffective. A new treatment exists that has been used successfully in other countries, but it has not yet been approved by the Food and Drug Administration. Do you think Jonas' insurance company should cover this experimental drug? Why or why not?

_____

_____

_____

_____

Chapter 15   Health and Life Insurance—Your Personal Security

15.5 Life Insurance

Key Terms Review

Define each of the following vocabulary terms.

1. death benefit_____

_____

2. beneficiary_____

3. term life insurance_____

_____

4. permanent life insurance_____

_____

Concepts Review

5. What is the purpose of life insurance?

_____

_____

6. How do life insurance companies calculate how much to charge you for the coverage they sell?

_____

_____

7. Why does the premium for term life insurance increase as your age increases?

_____

8. What is the major advantage of renewable term life insurance?

_____

9. How does permanent life insurance work?

_____

_____

_____

_____

Critical Thinking

10. Being able to convert to permanent life insurance without evidence of insurability would be a benefit to someone who had a terminal illness or practiced a dangerous hobby and would otherwise be unable to obtain life insurance. Do you think it is ethical to convert the policy if you know you are a high risk? Why or why not?

_____

_____

11. Why do you think that people today are less likely to choose life insurance as an investment option than stocks, bonds, or mutual funds?

_____

_____

_____

_____

Consumer Applications

12. Lucy is 32 years old and stays at home with her three children, ages 2, 4, and 6 months. Lucy does not have any life insurance but thinks that she should buy a policy. Her husband disagrees. Do you think that Lucy needs life insurance? Why or why not?

_____

_____

_____

_____

Chapter 16   Choose Services—When You Need Help

16.1 Health Care Providers

Key Terms Review

Define each of the following vocabulary terms.

1. internist _____

_____

2. family practitioner _____

_____

3. obstetrician/gynecologist (OB/GYN) _____

_____

_____

4. pediatrician _____

_____

5. board certified _____

_____

6. accreditation _____

_____

7. ophthalmologist _____

8. optometrist _____

_____

9. optician _____

Concepts Review

10. What are three qualities to look for in any doctor?

_____

11. How can you check a doctor's credentials?

_____

12. How do doctors become eligible to work in a hospital?

_____

13. What three questions should be addressed before choosing a hospital?

_____

_____

Critical Thinking

14. Why do you think it is difficult to get negative information from professional sources about a doctor?

_____

15. You go to a doctor who was highly recommended to you by several people in your community. You had your list of questions and concerns, but she acted as if they were unimportant and nothing to worry about. Would you be relieved that she considered you healthy? Or would you feel as if she didn't take you seriously? Does she have compassion and ability to communicate?

_____

_____

Consumer Applications

16. Claudia's primary care physician referred her to an orthopedist for her carpal tunnel syndrome. A good friend of hers had nothing positive to say about this doctor. She said the doctor was incompetent and had a horrible "bed-side" manner. Should Claudia accept her doctor's referral? What can she do to find out about the specialist?

_____

_____

_____

Chapter 16   Choose Services—When You Need Help

16.2 Legal Service Providers

Key Terms Review

Define each of the following vocabulary terms.

1. will_____

2. contingency fee_____

3. legal aid_____

    _____

4. public defender_____

    _____

5. mediator_____

    _____

Concepts Review

6. What professionals other than lawyers can handle legal matters for you?

    _____

    _____

    _____

7. What is often included in the charges that you should be aware of when a lawyer charges by the hour?

    _____

    _____

8. What are two types of percentage payment plans?

    _____

9. What should you be careful of if your lawyer is charging a contingency fee?

_____

_____

_____

10. What are some sources of low-cost legal services?

_____

_____

Critical Thinking

11. Why do you think states set monetary limits on lawsuits in small-claims court?

_____

_____

_____

12. Your landlord told you that if you wanted to paint your apartment, he would deduct the cost of the materials off your next month's rent. You present the bills with the rent check, and he threatens to sue you for unpaid rent, stating that he never agreed to pay for the materials. The amount in question is $85. What are your options? What do you think the outcome would be?

_____

_____

_____

_____

Consumer Applications

13. Rose is suing her former employer for $125,000. Her lawyer taking the case is charging $5,000 in expenses and a 30 percent contingency fee. If Rose wins the case, how much would she receive if her lawyer takes the expenses before the percentage? After the percentage?

_____

_____

Chapter 16   Choose Services—When You Need Help

16.3 Government Assistance

Key Terms Review

Define each of the following vocabulary terms.

1. welfare _____

   _____

2. poverty line _____

   _____

3. Temporary Assistance for Needy Family (TANF) _____

   _____

   _____

4. food stamps _____

   _____

5. Supplemental Security Income (SSI) _____

   _____

6. Women, Infants, and Children program (WIC) _____

   _____

   _____

7. Head Start _____

   _____

8. National School Lunch Program _____

   _____

9. public housing _____

10. social security_____

_____

11. unemployment compensation_____

_____

Concepts Review

12. What are the goals of TANF?

_____

_____

13. What are the main social security programs?

_____

_____

Critical Thinking

14. Why do you think the food stamp program converted from coupons to an electronic system?

_____

_____

Consumer Applications

15. Keith lost his job and filed for unemployment compensation. Keith said that he called in sick and his employer fired him. His employer said Keith called in sick frequently. Keith's benefits were denied. Do you think he was dismissed unfairly? What can Keith do?

_____

_____

_____

_____

Chapter 17   Global Economy—What It Means to You

17.1 The Nature of International Trade

Key Terms Review

Define each of the following vocabulary terms.

1. import _____

2. export _____

3. trade deficit _____

4. trade surplus _____

5. balance of trade _____

6. efficiency _____

7. absolute advantage _____

    _____

8. comparative advantage _____

    _____

9. tariff _____

10. quota _____

11. protectionism _____

12. North American Free Trade Agreement (NAFTA) _____

    _____

    _____

13. European Union (EU) _____

    _____

    _____

Concepts Review

14. How do countries benefit from trade?

_____

_____

15. What is a quota and why are quotas imposed?

_____

_____

_____

_____

16. What is the purpose of trade agreements?

_____

_____

Critical Thinking

17. How do you think the European Union affects the United States' ability to export?

_____

_____

_____

_____

Consumer Applications

18. Yuan owns a fabric store. His primary business is selling silk fabric from China. Last month, the government imposed a very high tariff on all imported fabric. How will this affect Yuan's business?

_____

_____

_____

Chapter 17   Global Economy—What It Means to You

17.2 U.S. Economy and World Trade

Key Terms Review

Define each of the following vocabulary terms.

1. exchange rate_____

2. floating exchange rates_____

   _____

Concepts Review

3. What products are the United States' most important exports?

   _____

   _____

4. Why do economists believe that international trade benefits the world overall?

   _____

   _____

   _____

   _____

   _____

5. Why might the public be less supportive of international trade?

   _____

   _____

   _____

   _____

   _____

6. What are some of the reasons businesses exchange one currency for another?

_____

_____

_____

7. How do exchange rates affect the prices of imports and exports?

_____

_____

8. How does the increase in the value of the U.S. dollar affect consumers?

_____

_____

_____

_____

Critical Thinking

9. Japanese manufacturers produce thousands of cars in the United States, employing American workers. Does this benefit the U.S. economy or the Japanese economy?

_____

_____

_____

10. Thirty percent of U.S. exports are services. Can you think of U.S. businesses that export services abroad?

_____

Consumer Applications

11. Dennis and Linda live close to the Canadian border. They decided to go out to dinner in Canada and paid $75 Canadian for their meal. The exchange rate is $0.75 Canadian dollars = $1 US dollar. How much did they pay in U.S. dollars?

_____

Chapter 17   Global Economy—What It Means to You

17.3 Government and the Economy

Key Terms Review

Define each of the following vocabulary terms.

1. gross domestic product (GDP)_____

_____

2. inflation_____

3. real GDP_____

4. Consumer Price Index (CPI)_____

_____

5. unemployment rate_____

_____

6. business cycle_____

7. recession_____

8. depression_____

9. fiscal policy_____

10. monetary policy_____

_____

Concepts Review

11. How is growing personal income related to economic conditions?

_____

_____

12. How do changes in business activity in one nation affect other nations?

_____

_____

_____

13. What are some of the ways the government can stimulate growth in a declining economy?

_____

_____

Critical Thinking

14. Why might the Federal Reserve Bank be concerned if the economy were growing too quickly?

_____

_____

_____

15. How does the health of the economy affect the decisions of business owners?

_____

_____

Consumer Applications

16. Deborah sells cars for a local dealership. How might government economic policy affect her job?

_____

_____

_____

_____

_____

Chapter 17   Global Economy—What It Means to You

17.4 It's a Global Economy

Key Terms Review

Define each of the following vocabulary terms.

1. multinational corporation (MNC)_____

   _____

Concepts Review

2. Is a global economy a recent development?

   _____

   _____

3. What important inventions have affected the world's economies?

   _____

4. Why do labor costs affect where multinational corporations choose to produce their products?

   _____

   _____

5. Does a company have to be a multinational corporation to do business globally?

   _____

   _____

6. What are some ways companies can enter foreign markets?

   _____

7. In what ways do the world's nations interact other than buying and selling products?

   _____

8. What are some global environmental problems?

_____

Critical Thinking

9. Who benefits when a corporation sells franchises to international markets?

_____

_____

_____

10. Suppose a researcher was hoping to win the Nobel Prize for Medicine. Why would she want to share knowledge and funding with another researcher working on the same project?

_____

_____

_____

_____

_____

Consumer Applications

11. Pascuala was surprised to learn that many items she uses on a daily basis are produced by multinational corporations. Her clothes, the fast-food restaurant where she eats lunch, her stereo equipment, the family car, and even the music she likes are but a few examples. She realizes that the global economy helps her live better and hopes that it helps others as well. Name ten companies that do business in the global marketplace, and tell what products or services each sells.

_____

_____

_____

_____